AMOS/HOSEA/
MICAH

A Call to
Justice

A Guided Discovery for Groups and Individuals

Joe Paprocki

LOYOLAPRESS.

CHICAGO

LOYOLAPRESS.

3441 N. ASHLAND AVENUE
CHICAGO, ILLINOIS 60657
(800) 621-1008
WWW.LOYOLABOOKS.ORG

Nihil Obstat	*Imprimatur*
Reverend John G. Lodge, S.S.L., S.T.D.	Reverend George J. Rassas
Censor Deputatus	Vicar General
June 1, 2005	Archdiocese of Chicago
	June 6, 2005

The *Nihil Obstat* and *Imprimatur* are official declarations that a book is free of doctrinal and moral error. No implication is contained therein that those who have granted the *Nihil Obstat* and *Imprimatur* agree with the content, opinions, or statements expressed. Nor do they assume any legal responsibility associated with publication.

Unless otherwise noted, the Scripture quotations contained herein are from the New Revised Standard Version Bible: Catholic Edition, copyright © 1993 and 1989 by the Division of Christian Education of the National Council of the Churches of Christ in the U.S.A. Used by permission. All rights reserved. Subheadings in Scripture quotations have been added by Joe Paprocki.

Excerpts from the English translation of *The Roman Missal* © 1973, International Committee on English in the Liturgy, Inc. (ICEL); excerpts from the English translation of *Rite of Christian Initiation of Adults* © 1985, ICEL. All rights reserved.

Interior design by Kay Hartmann/Communique Design
Illustration by Anni Betts

ISBN 0-8294-2118-1

Printed in the United States of America
06 07 08 09 10 11 Bang 10 9 8 7 6 5 4 3 2 1

Contents

How to Use This Guide

You might compare the Bible to a national park. The park is so large that you could spend months, even years, getting to know it. But a brief visit, if carefully planned, can be enjoyable and worthwhile. In a few hours you can drive through the park and pull over at a handful of sites. At each stop you can get out of the car, take a short trail through the woods, listen to the wind blowing through the trees, get a feel for the place.

In this book, we will read the books of three of the prophets: Amos, Hosea, and Micah. Because the excerpts are short, we will be able to take a leisurely walk through them, thinking carefully about what we are reading and what it means for our lives today.

This guide provides everything you need to explore Amos, Hosea, and Micah in six discussions—or to do a six-part exploration on your own. The introduction on page 6 will prepare you to get the most out of your reading. The weekly sections provide explanations that will help illuminate the meanings of the readings for your life. Equally important, each section supplies questions that will launch your group into fruitful discussion, helping you to both investigate the biblical text for yourself and learn from one another. If you're using the book by yourself, the questions will spur your personal reflection.

Each discussion is meant to be a *guided discovery.*

Guided. None of us is equipped to read the Bible without help. We read the Bible *for* ourselves but not *by* ourselves. Scripture was written to be understood and applied in the community of faith. So each week you'll find background and explanations in "A Guide to the Reading," which draws on the work of both modern biblical scholars and Christian writers of the past. The guide will help you grasp the meanings of Amos, Hosea, and Micah. Think of it as a friendly park ranger who points out noteworthy details and explains what you're looking at so you can appreciate things for yourself.

Discovery. The purpose is for *you* to interact with Amos, Hosea, and Micah. "Questions for Careful Reading" is a tool to help you dig into the text and examine it carefully. "Questions for Application" will help you consider what these words mean for your life here and now. Each week concludes with an "Approach to Prayer" section that helps you respond to God's word. Supplementary "Living Tradition" and "Saints in the Making" sections offer the thoughts and experiences of Christians past and present. By showing what the messages of Amos, Hosea, and Micah have meant to others, these sections will help you consider what they mean for you.

How long are the discussion sessions? We've assumed you will have about an hour and a half when you get together. If you have less time, you'll find that most of the elements can be shortened somewhat.

Is homework necessary? You will get the most out of your discussions if you read the weekly material and prepare answers to the questions in advance of each meeting. If participants are not able to prepare, have someone read the "Guide to the Reading" sections aloud to the group at the points where they appear.

What about leadership? If you happen to have a world-class biblical scholar in your group, by all means ask him or her to lead the discussions. In the absence of any professional Scripture scholars, or even accomplished amateur biblical scholars, you can still have a first-class Bible discussion. Choose two or three people to take turns as facilitators, and have everyone read "Suggestions for Bible Discussion Groups" (page 76) before beginning.

Does everyone need a guide? a Bible? Everyone in the group will need his or her own copy of this book. It contains the passages from Amos, Hosea, and Micah, so a Bible is not absolutely necessary—but each participant will find it useful to have one. You should have at least one Bible on hand for your discussions (see page 80 for recommendations.)

How do we get started? Before you begin, take a look at the suggestions for Bible discussion groups (page 76) or individuals (page 79).

Minding Our Own Business?

In Charles Dickens's classic *A Christmas Carol*, Ebenezer Scrooge is visited by the spirit of his former business partner, Jacob Marley, who has come to alert Scrooge to the three spirits who will visit him in an attempt to save his soul. When Scrooge asks Marley why he is laden down with chains and irons, Marley explains that he is wearing the chains he "forged in life" as a punishment for not making better use of his time on earth. Scrooge protests, "But you were always a good man of business, Jacob." To which Marley laments, "Business! . . . Mankind was my business! The common welfare was my business; charity, mercy, forbearance, and benevolence, were, all, my business. The dealings of my trade were but a drop of water in the comprehensive ocean of my business!"

For Jacob Marley, it was too late. For Ebenezer Scrooge, it was not. Neither is it for us.

Luckily for us, the message that the spirit of Jacob Marley brought to Ebenezer Scrooge is alive and well, not in the form of a specter but in the living word of the biblical prophets. In many ways, Jacob Marley's message echoes the challenging message that the prophets issued to the people of Israel. Today, more than ever, we need to hear this same message, namely that humankind is our business, "the common welfare" is our business, "charity, mercy, forbearance, and benevolence" are all our business.

The prophets whose writings we are about to read—Amos, Hosea, and Micah—tell us that other peoples' business is our business when those people are suffering economic hardship and oppression. The prophets go further still, pointing out that the reason some people are suffering is because of the way others conduct their business. Just as Jesus' parable of the rich man and Lazarus (Luke 16:19–31) teaches us to pay attention to the poor beggar at our gate, Amos, Hosea, and Micah call us to open up our eyes to the needs of others who are suffering due to the way we conduct business. Reading the prophets' words is an opportunity to examine how, even without our realizing it, our lifestyle may have a negative impact on the lives of others.

To grasp the prophets' message, a little background is helpful. Amos, Micah, and Hosea lived some seven centuries before Christ. Some two hundred years earlier, the Israelites had a united and prosperous kingdom ruled by David and then by his son Solomon. Although Solomon's reign was characterized by peace and prosperity, his death unleashed dissension and unrest because of heavy taxation and forced labor. His son Rehoboam was unable to maintain unity, and the kingdom split in two—a northern kingdom called Israel, with its capital in Samaria, and a southern kingdom called Judah, with its capital in Jerusalem. With this division, of course, came weakness—something that did not go unnoticed by neighboring rivals such as Egypt and Assyria. Israel and Judah struggled to maintain their independence from these foreign threats, sometimes trying to play them off against each other. Finally, in the year 721 BC, the northern kingdom was invaded and conquered by the Assyrians. As was the practice of warfare at the time, the Assyrians deported many of the inhabitants of the northern kingdom (now known as the "lost tribes" of Israel) and replaced them with foreign colonists. The southern kingdom remained autonomous for another 130 years until the Babylonian invasion of 587. The Babylonians destroyed the temple in Jerusalem, the focal point of God's presence among the people, and took the king and leading citizens into captivity. The people lost everything: land, temple, and kingship. This began the period known as the Exile.

It was during the period leading up to the collapse of the northern and southern kingdoms that Amos, Hosea, and Micah spoke the word of God to God's people. In contrast to what is often thought, biblical prophets were not concerned with foretelling the distant future. Rather, they were mainly concerned about what was going to happen to the people of their own day. To help people understand where they were heading, the prophets directed people's attention to the past. They reminded people that some five hundred years earlier God had led them from slavery in Egypt to freedom in the Promised Land. The exodus story demonstrated that God had remained faithful to the promise he had made earlier to Abraham to "give to you, and to your offspring after you, the land where you are now an alien, all the land of Canaan, for a perpetual holding" (Genesis 17:8). The prophets also reminded the people of the social justice that God had required of them when he brought them out of Egypt and made a covenant with them. The prophets observed frequent and blatant disregard for the social justice that God mandated in his law; they felt compelled to point out these transgressions and call the people of Israel to return to faithfulness to the covenant lest they face dire consequences. Because people do not like to be told how to conduct their business, the warning of the prophets went largely unheeded. It was partly owing to the loss of social justice that the kingdoms of Israel and Judah deteriorated and eventually collapsed.

For the people of Judah who were driven off to Babylonia—in present-day Iraq—the Exile was a devastating experience that posed a serious problem for their faith. They faced the possibility that this was indeed the end for them as a people. To some, it seemed that their God had been defeated, that the covenant was broken forever, and that they were abandoned in a foreign land. During this period of exile, however, the Judeans remained faithful to God, in no small part due to prophets who assured them that God had not abandoned them. When Cyrus of Persia decreed that the Judeans could return home in 538 BC, thousands chose to do so, buoyed by their faith, filled with hope, and eager to rebuild their homeland.

It is important to note that the books of Amos, Hosea, and Micah were not compiled until after the people returned from exile. When the editors put these books together, they included not only the warnings of the three preexilic prophets, but also messages of hope that later prophets spoke to buoy the spirits of those returning from the Exile and attempting to rebuild their lives. These prophetic messages reminded the Jewish people to look to the future while keeping their eyes on the past, recalling God's great deeds and the intimacy their ancestors shared with God during times of fidelity. Their words bear the same message for us today.

Getting back to Dickens's A Christmas Carol, we find Ebenezer Scrooge, now painfully aware of his own shortcomings and selfishness, begging the Ghost of Christmas Yet to Come to offer him some glimmer of hope, namely, the possibility of repentance. "'Men's courses will foreshadow certain ends, to which, if persevered in, they must lead,' said Scrooge. 'But if the courses be departed from, the ends will change. Say it is thus with what you show me!'" Scrooge rightly concludes that by changing courses the ends may be changed. The prophets Amos, Hosea, and Micah offer this same proposition: a changed way of living will result in a future not of doom but of promise. Just as the spirits that visit Scrooge point out specific situations for him to face up to, the prophets point out specific transgressions for the people to come face-to-face with. Let's take a closer look at each of these prophets to see how their message called people to depart from their present courses in favor of a preferred end.

The prophet Amos does not mince words but speaks in a blunt, sometimes offensive style. His purpose is to provoke people to action by delivering accusations of wrongdoing and divine judgments on those who are violating God's call to justice. Perhaps Amos learned to speak in such a gruff manner in his first career as a shepherd in Judah. Shepherds were in many ways like cowboys, grizzly outdoorsmen who were unpolished in the ways of tact. Amos, although from the southern kingdom, pronounced his word in the northern kingdom between 786 and 746 BC. He was not a professional prophet in the sense that he was not trained to assume the role. In fact, Amos took great pains to distance himself from those he considered to be career prophets. This was his way of emphasizing that he had been called to prophesy directly by God—in contrast to the professional prophets, whose calling he questioned.

In his prophecies, Amos indicts just about every nation in the region, but he saves his harshest criticism for Israel, accusing her of blatant injustice and idolatry. Amos tells the people of Israel that they can expect a "day of the Lord" (5:18)—a day when God will bring justice to the earth. But, contrary to their expectations, this will not be a day of deliverance for them from their enemies but a terrible day—a day of darkness, not light, a day when their own injustice will be brought to an end. Amos's goal was not to condemn people but to call them to salvation, to reform their lives and their society in line with God's justice so that they might experience his help again.

We are always confounded when we witness one person unconditionally loving another person whose faults are blatantly obvious to the world. "What does he see in her?" we may ask, or "How does she stay with him?" People may have talked like that about Hosea and his wife, Gomer, who was unfaithful to him. In his own difficult marriage, Hosea saw a similarity to the relationship between God and his unfaithful people. Hosea likens Israel to an unfaithful spouse to highlight the sinfulness of God's people. Hosea emphasizes the undying and unwavering faithfulness and love that God has for his people, despite their unfaithfulness, by comparing God's faithfulness to Hosea's own faithfulness to Gomer. Like Amos, Hosea preached his word in the northern kingdom between 786 and 746 BC. Hosea taught that, just as he could not give up on his wife, Gomer, even after she had strayed, God could never give up on his people, Israel, even though they had strayed into idolatry and ruthless oppression of the poor. As in Amos, Hosea's harsh indictment of the people is for the purpose of calling them back into a loving relationship with God and one another. While Hosea can often be as blunt as Amos, his comparison of God's relationship with his people to a marriage includes a tenderness that is absent from Amos's prophecies.

The prophet Micah sought to maintain an alertness in the people of Israel and Judah. For Micah, there is a reward up ahead, but that reward will be forfeited by those who neglect their responsibilities. Micah indicts those who exploit the poor as well as those priests and prophets who are mired in corruption. He warns them of the punishment that they will face if they do not heed his words. Through it all, however, Micah sees a light at the end of the tunnel and accompanies each of his judgments with the promise of hope for a better future. The name *Micah* means "Who is like?"— short for "Who is like God?" This is an appropriate name for him because his prophetic word is designed to help people understand what it means to truly be godlike. In his indictments, Micah points out how ungodlike the people have been. Micah attempts to show how they can live in godlike fashion by loving justice, doing kindness, and walking humbly with God.

The prophets raise an important question: What do we mean by justice? "Blessed are those who hunger and thirst for righteousness, for they will be filled," Jesus declared in the Sermon on the Mount (Matthew 5:6). The Greek word for "righteousness" can also be translated as "justice." We sometimes think of justice as a strictly legal term, for example, when we say that someone who is punished for an offense has been "brought to justice." This understanding tends to equate justice with retribution. The Bible, however, understands "righteousness," or "justice," as much more than this. While God does bring retribution on those who do wrong, he also expresses justice through his faithfulness, trustworthiness, and compassion. To say that God is just means that you can always count on him to do the right thing—to show compassion and mercy in all situations. With this understanding, the people of Israel prayed for God's justice, meaning that they prayed that God would stand by them and do the right thing, being compassionate and merciful toward them. The people, in turn, recognized that God expected them to deal with one another in the same way, namely, by respecting people's rights, by fulfilling their obligations to one another, by showing compassion and mercy to others in all situations, and by caring for those who are in need of any kind. With this understanding of justice, we realize that God's call to be just means a summons to practice justice in every aspect of our daily lives.

To help us live so that justice may prevail in our world today, the bishops of the United States wrote *Sharing Catholic Social Teaching: Challenges and Directions,* which outlines seven principles of social justice in Catholic teaching.

- ♦ **Dignity of the Human Person.** All human life is sacred, and all people must be respected and valued over material goods. We are called to ask whether our actions as a society respect or threaten the life and dignity of the human person.

- **Call to Family, Community, and Participation.**
  People have not only a right but also a duty to participate in
  society. As the principal social institution, the family must be
  supported so that people can participate in society, build a
  community spirit, and promote the well-being of all, especially
  those who are poor and vulnerable.
- **Rights and Responsibilities.** Every person has a right to
  those things required for a decent human life, such as food,
  clothing, and shelter. As Catholics, it is our responsibility to
  protect these basic human rights in order to achieve a healthy
  society.
- **Option for the Poor and Vulnerable.** In our world,
  some people are very rich while, at the same time, many are
  extremely poor. As Catholics, we are called to pay special
  attention to the needs of the poor by defending and promoting
  their dignity and by assisting them in meeting their immediate
  material needs.
- **Dignity of Work and the Rights of Workers.** The
  basic rights of all workers are to be respected: the right to
  productive work, fair wages, and private property, and the right
  to organize, join unions, and pursue economic opportunity.
  Catholics believe that the economy is meant to serve people;
  work is not merely a way to make a living but is an important
  means by which we participate in God's creation.
- **Solidarity.** Because God is our Father, we are all brothers
  and sisters, with the responsibility to care for one another.
  Solidarity is the attitude that leads Christians to share
  spiritual and material goods, uniting rich and poor, weak and
  strong; solidarity helps to create a society that recognizes that
  we all depend upon one another.
- **Care for God's Creation.** God is the creator of all
  people and all things, and he wants us to enjoy his creation.
  The responsibility to care for all that God has made is a
  requirement of our faith.

Physical fitness experts will tell you that, while exercise should not cause pain, there can be little benefit or muscle growth without physical stress. Muscles that are not accustomed to stress react painfully at first. For this reason, many people who are out of shape avoid exercise because they cannot get beyond the initial pain. In much the same way, we sometimes avoid spiritual growth because of the initial pain of conversion. More often than not, conversion is a call to mobilize spiritual muscles that have been lying dormant. Spiritual growth often involves recognizing sins of omission and the harm of what we have failed to do.

Amos, Hosea, and Micah call us to spiritual growth, since spirituality is manifested in the way we act toward our neighbors. Their initial call may cause us great distress, because we realize we are being called to flex spiritual muscles that have either never been used or have atrophied. If we heed the words of the prophets, recognize our weakness, and begin flexing the muscles of compassion, unselfishness, mercy, forgiveness, and justice, we may feel some pain. But the benefits will be a spiritually healthy relationship with God and neighbor, leading to a world in which justice prevails.

The prophets' call to justice is at the very heart of what it means for us to be disciples of Christ today. At the Last Supper, Jesus instituted the Eucharist with these words: "This is my body, which is given for you. Do this in remembrance of me" (Luke 22:19). John's Gospel tells us that at the Last Supper, Jesus got up from the table and washed the feet of his disciples, then told them, "You also should do as I have done to you" (John 13:15). When Jesus told us to "do this" in his memory, he was telling us to *do* much more than celebrate the Last Supper meal—the Mass. He was telling us to give ourselves to others as he gave himself for us. We learn what it is that we are to *do* in this way of life, in part, from the powerful words of the prophets in Scripture, who call us to live in such a way that justice may prevail.

GOD'S WAKE-UP CALL

Questions to Begin

15 minutes
Use a question or two to get warmed up for the reading.

1 Are you a morning person? What does it take to wake you up and get you started in the morning?

2 If you could choose any place at all, where would you get away to in the middle of summer? in the middle of winter?

5 minutes
Read the passage aloud. Let individuals take turns reading sections.

The Reading: Amos 2:6–8; 3:1–8, 10–15

Indictment Handed Down

> 2:6 Thus says the LORD:
> For three transgressions of Israel,
>   and for four, I will not revoke the punishment;
> because they sell the righteous for silver,
>   and the needy for a pair of sandals—
> 7 they who trample the head of the poor into the dust of
>   the earth,
>   and push the afflicted out of the way;
> father and son go in to the same girl,
>   so that my holy name is profaned;
> 8 they lay themselves down beside every altar
>   on garments taken in pledge;
> and in the house of their God they drink
>   wine bought with fines they imposed.

God Means Business

3:1 Hear this word that the LORD has spoken against you, O people of Israel, against the whole family that I brought up out of the land of Egypt:

> 2 You only have I known
>   of all the families of the earth;
> therefore I will punish you
>   for all your iniquities.

> 3 Do two walk together
>   unless they have made an appointment?
> 4 Does a lion roar in the forest,
>   when it has no prey?
> Does a young lion cry out from its den,
>   if it has caught nothing?
> 5 Does a bird fall into a snare on the earth,
>   when there is no trap for it?
> Does a snare spring up from the ground,

when it has taken nothing?
6 Is a trumpet blown in a city,
    and the people are not afraid?
  Does disaster befall a city,
    unless the LORD has done it?
7 Surely the Lord GOD does nothing,
    without revealing his secret
    to his servants the prophets.
8 The lion has roared;
    who will not fear?
  The Lord GOD has spoken;
    who can but prophesy? . . .

Heading for Trouble

10 They do not know how to do right, says the LORD,
    those who store up violence and robbery in their
        strongholds.
11 Therefore thus says the Lord GOD:
  An adversary shall surround the land,
    and strip you of your defense;
    and your strongholds shall be plundered.
12 Thus says the LORD: As the shepherd rescues from the
mouth of the lion two legs, or a piece of an ear, so shall the people of
Israel who live in Samaria be rescued, with the corner of a couch and
part of a bed.

13 Hear, and testify against the house of Jacob,
    says the Lord GOD, the God of hosts:
14 On the day I punish Israel for its transgressions,
    I will punish the altars of Bethel,
  and the horns of the altar shall be cut off
    and fall to the ground.
15 I will tear down the winter house as well as the
        summer house;
    and the houses of ivory shall perish,
  and the great houses shall come to an end,
                                    says the LORD.

10 minutes
Choose questions according to your interest and time.

1 The words of Amos might be described as a wake-up call. Who is Amos trying to wake up?

2 In 2:6–8, what "transgressions," or wrongs, is Amos attempting to call his listeners' attention to?

3 In 3:1–2, what reason does God give for being particularly hurt?

4 What seems to be the point of the questions in 3:3–6?

5 What feeling are you left with in 3:13–15?

A Guide to the Reading

If participants have not read this section already, read it aloud. Otherwise go on to "Questions for Application."

2:6–8. To get the attention of his listeners, Amos uses a very effective approach. In the section before our reading begins (1:3–2:5), he has publicly denounced the sins against humanity committed by a number of neighboring nations, all of which are hostile to Israel. Like a crowd at a political convention, the listeners to Amos's tirade most likely cheered the condemnation of their enemies. But then Amos throws a powerful punch: he includes Israel in the list. Imagine the shock to Amos's audience as he mentions Israel and, instead of acquitting her, condemns her injustices in the harshest terms. By including Israel in his list of nations guilty of sins against humanity, Amos is showing that Israel's privileged status as a chosen people does not give her a license to violate the requirements of justice.

What exactly is Israel guilty of? According to Amos, some people in Israel are growing in prosperity at the expense of the poor. Amos points out that the wealthy are selling people into slavery "for silver . . . for a pair of sandals" (2:6) by brutally enforcing laws aimed at collecting debts from those who do not have enough to meet their needs. In 2:7, Amos points out that the deplorable sexual practices of some people are acts that profane God's holy name, a profanation that occurs anytime they act in a way that is contrary to what God's name stands for—namely, justice, compassion, and mercy. In 2:8, Amos talks about "garments taken in pledge." He is referring to a practice by which a lender takes the outer cloak belonging to the borrower as a sign of the borrower's pledge to repay (Exodus 22:25–27; Deuteronomy 24:12–13). This cloak is to be returned at sunset so that the borrower can use it as a blanket to keep warm at night. Amos points out that the wealthy are not only keeping these cloaks but are reclining on them, committing sexual sins while under the influence. In the meantime, the poor are freezing without their cloaks.

3:1–8. Today's fascination with courtroom drama is nothing new. Amos uses the image of a courtroom to make his next point. As chapter 3 begins, Amos is presenting a lawsuit against the people of Israel. This is a covenant lawsuit, meaning that God will argue that he has kept the promise of faithfulness he made when he entered a covenant with the people of Israel but that they have reneged on their agreement to obey him. The passage follows a legal pattern: the defendant is summoned, the crimes are listed, the judge speaks, and the verdict and punishment are handed down.

Despite the accusatory tone of 3:1, God expresses his favor toward Israel in the first part of 3:2. *Perhaps,* the listeners might think, *God is going to exonerate us.* No such luck. Instead, God announces that only punishment will follow. His point is that their status as the chosen people does not grant them immunity from prosecution for their crimes against their neighbors but rather lays on them a greater responsibility to treat others justly.

Apparently, some of Amos's listeners dismiss his prophecies as empty ranting. So, in 3:3–6, he defends himself, using a list of rhetorical questions. To his listeners, these questions would be as sarcastic as the familiar contemporary question "Is the pope Catholic?" Amos poses these questions to illustrate the point that nothing happens by chance. Every effect has a cause. "Well," Amos declares, "cause and effect is at work right now. God's inspiration is the cause of my prophecies of judgment. So take warning, and change your ways!" (see 3:7–8).

3:10–15. The punishment that Amos warns of is not at all attractive—defeat at the hands of the Assyrians, a ferocious military enemy. Amos makes it very clear that God does not impose this punishment arbitrarily. It is an inevitable effect of the people's own sinful decisions and actions. As long as the wealthy of Israel fail to protect the poor and vulnerable of their own society, they cannot expect to find protection for themselves from the dangers that surround them.

As far as Amos is concerned, the trial is over, and the verdict has been handed down: guilty as charged. The punishment, though harsh, fits the crime. The Israelites are guilty of a serious breach of contract, namely, appalling social injustices (2:6–8; 3:10) and cruel economic inequities. The poor are reduced to slavery (2:6), while the wealthy enjoy luxury housing (3:15). The Israelites have broken the covenant with God, while God has faithfully upheld his end of the bargain.

Questions for Application

40 minutes
Choose questions according to your interest and time.

1 In light of Amos's words that you have read thus far, what might he be saying to you about:
- ♦ your participation in parish life?
- ♦ your way of handling matters in the workplace?
- ♦ your pattern of relating to family members?
- ♦ your participation in civic affairs, both locally and nationally?

In these areas, what have you done well? Where can you be doing better?

2 In your parish, community, nation, or the world, who are the people who are striving to send a message regarding injustice? What specific actions are they calling people to? Are others listening and responding? Are you listening and responding? Is there a wake-up call that you have heard but have failed to act on?

3 Based on these passages from Amos, what is God most concerned with? In what ways are God's concerns applicable today?

4 In addition to the economically impoverished, who are the poor in our society? How are the poor being trampled upon in society today? in other places in the world? What have you done or can you do to address the needs of the poor in your community? in the nation? in the world?

5 When Amos speaks of God's name being "profaned," he is speaking about acts of social injustice. How is God's name being profaned today? What can you personally do to bring honor to God's name?

6 Amos threatens that God will punish Israelite society if evils are not corrected. What "punishments" are we living with today as a result of not addressing social ills in the past? What "punishments" does society face in the future if we do not address some of today's social ills?

7 After learning about some of Amos's strategies described in these passages, what strategies would you say work best for issuing a wake-up call about injustice in today's society? What are the areas that we should focus our efforts on?

The first step in listening to the word God speaks to us through Scripture is to begin reading the Bible, and to begin reading it *daily*.

George Martin, *Reading Scripture as the Word of God*

Approach to Prayer

15 minutes
Use this approach—or create your own!

♦ Invite participants to pause in silent reflection, calling to mind the ways that they have failed to act for those who are suffering injustice. Pause for a moment in silence. Then pray the Confiteor aloud together:

I confess to almighty God,
and to you, my brothers and
    sisters,
that I have sinned through my
    own fault
in my thoughts and in my words,
in what I have done,
and what I have failed to do;
and I ask blessed Mary, ever
    virgin,
all the angels and saints,
and you, my brothers and sisters,
to pray for me to the Lord our
    God.

Living Tradition

Consistently Pro-Life

This section is a supplement for individual reading.

Every week, Deacon Richard Kulleck of the Most Holy Redeemer Parish in Evergreen Park, Illinois, coordinates the efforts of volunteers at a Public Action to Deliver Shelter facility on the Southwest Side of Chicago, providing hospitality, meals, and shelter to those who are homeless. Like the many Christians who struggle against abortion, euthanasia, military aggression, capital punishment, sexual exploitation, and unjust distribution of resources, Deacon Rich is pro-life.

Being pro-life is often equated with the struggle to end abortion and, indeed, this effort is at the very heart of the pro-life movement. However, to be pro-life is to be consistent in our approach to all life issues, from the cradle to the grave. The late Cardinal Joseph Bernardin of Chicago articulated with particular clarity what it means to have a "consistent ethic of life." Cardinal Bernardin used the image of a "seamless garment" to teach us that all life issues, while not equal, are intimately linked. Having a consistent ethic of life does not require every individual or group to struggle equally for all life issues. However, while struggling for a particular life issue, someone who has a consistent pro-life ethic will be sensitive to other life issues. This is not to say that all life issues are morally equivalent. Rather, it is to affirm that all life issues are linked by a common thread: our belief that all human life is sacred.

People like Deacon Rich and the myriad of other people who struggle to uphold the dignity of life help us to see that having a consistent ethic of life leads not only to individual acts of charity but also to involvement in political life. In the words of Cardinal Bernardin, "When human life is considered 'cheap' or easily expendable in one area, eventually nothing is held as sacred and all lives are in jeopardy." Catholics are called upon to be pro-life by consistently standing in defense of the dignity of human life, beginning with the life of the unborn and continuing to the grave.

TOUGH LOVE

Questions to Begin

15 minutes
Use a question or two to get warmed up for the reading.

1 What is your favorite portrayal of a courtroom lawyer from a TV show or a movie? What qualities and skills did this lawyer use to win over juries?

2 When you were a child, what kind of unfairness bothered you most?

5 minutes
Read the passage aloud. Let individuals take turns reading
sections.

The Reading: Micah 1:2–5; 2:1–2; 3:1–5, 8–12

Now Hear This!

1:2 Hear, you peoples, all of you;
    listen, O earth, and all that is in it;
  and let the Lord GOD be a witness against you,
    the Lord from his holy temple.
3 For lo, the LORD is coming out of his place,
    and will come down and tread upon the high places
      of the earth.
4 Then the mountains will melt under him
    and the valleys will burst open,
  like wax near the fire,
    like waters poured down a steep place.
5 All this is for the transgression of Jacob
    and for the sins of the house of Israel. . . .

2:1 Alas for those who devise wickedness
    and evil deeds on their beds!
  When the morning dawns, they perform it,
    because it is in their power.
2 They covet fields, and seize them;
    houses, and take them away;
  they oppress householder and house,
    people and their inheritance. . . .

Disregard for Human Life

3:1 And I said:
  Listen, you heads of Jacob
    and rulers of the house of Israel!
  Should you not know justice?—
2 you who hate the good and love the evil,
  who tear the skin off my people,
    and the flesh off their bones;
3 who eat the flesh of my people,
    flay their skin off them,

break their bones in pieces,
  and chop them up like meat in a kettle,
  like flesh in a caldron.

⁴ Then they will cry to the LORD,
  but he will not answer them;
he will hide his face from them at that time,
  because they have acted wickedly.

Tell It Like It Is

⁵ Thus says the LORD concerning the prophets
  who lead my people astray,
who cry "Peace"
  when they have something to eat,
but declare war against those
  who put nothing into their mouths. . . .
⁸ But as for me, I am filled with power,
  with the spirit of the LORD,
  and with justice and might,
to declare to Jacob his transgression
  and to Israel his sin.

⁹ Hear this, you rulers of the house of Jacob
  and chiefs of the house of Israel,
who abhor justice
  and pervert all equity,
¹⁰ who build Zion with blood
  and Jerusalem with wrong!
¹¹ Its rulers give judgment for a bribe,
  its priests teach for a price,
  its prophets give oracles for money;
yet they lean upon the LORD and say,
  "Surely the LORD is with us!
  No harm shall come upon us."
¹² Therefore because of you
  Zion shall be plowed as a field;
Jerusalem shall become a heap of ruins,
  and the mountain of the house a wooded height.

10 minutes
Choose questions according to your interest and time.

1 In 1:2–4, which images would lend themselves well to special effects in a Hollywood movie?

2 What feelings might 1:4–5 have provoked in Micah's listeners?

3 In 2:2 and 3:2–3, what sins is Micah drawing attention to?

4 What does Micah see as the main problem with other prophets of his age? What is the difference between Micah and these other prophets?

A Guide to the Reading

If participants have not read this section already, read it aloud. Otherwise go on to "Questions for Application."

1:2–5; 2:1–2. Just in case Amos was not enough to wake us up, now we have Micah! Like Amos, Micah borrows a scene from judicial reality and acts like a bailiff who announces, in essence, that court is in session ("Hear, you peoples"—1:2). Micah heralds the very regal entrance of the one who will be "witness" (1:2), prosecutor, and judge: the Lord God. It becomes immediately clear that God has come to these proceedings to administer judgment. The Lord's entrance, complete with the melting and collapsing of the mountains and the bursting of valleys, signals that it is a time for transformation.

Beginning with 1:5, Micah lays out the evidence against the people of Israel, announcing their crimes. And just what are the sins of Israel that Micah lays bare? Chapter 2:1–2 reveals to us that the wealthy landowners are devising ways to force small landowners into debt so that they can then take their land from them. Here we see Micah articulating God's compassion for the poor and vulnerable of society, mostly rural people, who are being taken advantage of by the urban landowners. Micah is very clear that these misdeeds are being undertaken brazenly, in broad daylight. The condemnation of these misdeeds, while directed at the people of Israel, continues to speak to us today, even though our social, economic, and political landscapes are quite different from Israel's, seven centuries before Christ. Micah's words were originally intended for people living in a society that was primarily agrarian, with small concentrations of wealthy landowners living in cities. Although our social landscape is vastly different, the issue of the distribution of wealth remains important. Micah's message now speaks a powerful message to the entire world, in which it is estimated that 20 percent of the population currently holds 85 percent of the wealth.

3:1–4. Micah resumes his indictment with a grim image that indicates the seriousness of the injustice—it involves the destruction of human beings. Using very graphic language, Micah draws on actions performed in the slaughter and butchering of animals in order to characterize the ways in which the leaders of Israel were tearing peoples' lives apart. Micah draws attention to this wholesale disregard for human life in order to justify the severe penalties that God is planning to exact. Verse 4 reveals that punishment—the apparent absence and silence of God—is at hand.

3:5, 8–12. God's "lawsuit" now becomes even more specific as Micah moves from indicting the powerful in Israel (2:1) to singling out those prophets who are leading the people astray (3:5). Micah obviously has little respect for these diviners who pay too much attention to the opinion polls, changing their message depending on which way the wind is blowing and simply telling people what they want to hear. Micah condemns them for reassuring the people and telling them that everything is okay when it is obvious that all is not well in their society. Micah makes a connection between false prophecy and injustice as he points out that the false prophets are telling the exploiters that they have nothing to fear from their injustices and that God will keep them secure no matter how badly they treat their neighbors.

At this point (3:8–11), Micah declares the purpose of his own ministry. In 3:8, he states his credentials as someone who is "filled with power, with the spirit of the Lord." His purpose is "to declare to Jacob his transgression and to Israel his sin" (3:8). Unlike the other prophets, Micah is not concerned with his own well-being or popularity. He proves this by predicting the downfall of Jerusalem—a concept not only shocking to his listeners but even blasphemous. To the Israelites, the temple in Jerusalem and the city itself were viewed as indestructible because of God's presence there. Micah breaks through this complacent illusion and tells the people that the fact that they are chosen is no guarantee of unconditional protection: God will not protect those who commit injustice, even if they have the temple where God promised to make himself especially present.

Questions for Application

40 minutes
Choose questions according to your interest and time.

1 Micah says that poor people are being taken advantage of in his society. In what ways are poor people being taken advantage of in today's society? Are the reasons for poverty the same? different? What can you do about it?

2 What practices and policies in our own economy worsen poverty? In what ways might your own economic habits contribute to these problems?

3 Micah says that when those who do injustice call out to God, God will not answer them. When was a time that you called out to God and felt that he wasn't there? What kinds of punishments do we bring upon ourselves as a result of our actions toward others?

4 Micah criticizes the people of Israel for their complacency despite the presence of neighbors in need. Reflect on complacency—on feeling self-satisfied despite the needs of other people. Is it an attitude you slip into? How can a person become more aware of his or her own complacency?

5 In 3:1–3, Micah exposes the blatant disregard for human life In Israel. What practices in our society display a blatant disregard for human life?

6 Micah raises the issue of prophets' credibility in 3:11. The complacent prophets who oppose him are not to be believed because they take money for their prophecies. Is this an issue today? How do you assess the credibility of people who claim to speak with God's authority about social ills?

7 What injustice especially concerns you? How can you learn more about the problem? What could you do to bring it to others' attention? What kind of remedies might improve the situation?

Become an apprentice of the Bible. Ordinary people can reach a good level of understanding, but it costs: The Bible yields its riches to those who give themselves to the search for understanding.

Michael Cameron, *At Home with the Word*

Approach to Prayer

15 minutes
Use this approach—or create your own!

♦ Invite the participants to pray for the poor and for the wisdom and direction to work for justice. Ask participants to offer intentions for those who are suffering, as well as for people who are working for justice. Close by praying the following words attributed to St. Ignatius of Loyola:

Love consists in sharing
what one has
and what one is
with those one loves.
Love ought to show itself in
        deeds
more than in words.

Saints in the Making

Rosa Parks: A Prophet of Action

This section is a supplement for individual reading.

When we think of modern-day prophets, we may think of people like Dr. Martin Luther King Jr., a visionary who became a voice for the struggle for racial justice, economic justice, and nonviolence. Like the prophets Amos, Micah, and Hosea, he envisioned a society transformed by a commitment to justice, dignity, and peace.

Dr. King was a master of words, a great orator who stirred people to consider new possibilities. Prophecy, however, is not to be thought of as strictly an oral exercise. Throughout Scripture, prophets demonstrate the intimate link between words and actions. Dr. King knew well the power of actions, and he inspired thousands upon thousands of people to take action, nonviolently, to bring about change. In that spirit, the civil rights movement took shape in both words and actions. One prophet of the movement was a woman who spoke little but made a profound statement through her action: Rosa Parks. One day in 1955, in Montgomery, Alabama, Rosa Parks refused a bus driver's demand to give up her seat to a white person. She was arrested and fined for violating a city racial-segregation ordinance, but her act of defiance inspired a movement that eventually changed a nation. Mrs. Parks's action led to the formation of the Montgomery Improvement Association, led by the young pastor of the Dexter Avenue Baptist Church, the Reverend Dr. Martin Luther King Jr., who was chosen to lead a boycott of the city-owned bus company. The boycott, inspired by Rosa Parks's action, lasted 382 days and led to a Supreme Court decision that struck down the Montgomery ordinance under which she had been fined, thus outlawing racial segregation in public transportation throughout the nation.

Although Mrs. Parks had been weary from her long day's work as a seamstress, it is obvious that she was much wearier of living in a society that denied her worth, a society that had enslaved black Americans and continued to oppress them. She had the same dream that Dr. King had—of a society where all people would be treated equally, regardless of the color of their skin. Dr. King used powerful, prophetic words to proclaim this vision. Rosa Parks proclaimed it with a powerful, prophetic action.

SECOND CHANCES

Questions to Begin

15 minutes
Use a question or two to get warmed up for the reading.

1   If you were an alien from another planet seeking an understanding of the concept of love, what would you conclude from watching TV and movies?

2   What is missing from these depictions of love?

Read the passage aloud. Let individuals take turns reading sections.

The Reading: Hosea 2:7, 14–20; 6:4–9, 11; 7:8, 11–13, 16

Making Up Is Hard to Do

2:7 She shall pursue her lovers,
    but not overtake them;
and she shall seek them,
    but shall not find them.
Then she shall say, "I will go
    and return to my first husband,
    for it was better with me then than now."...

14 Therefore, I will now allure her,
    and bring her into the wilderness,
    and speak tenderly to her.
15 From there I will give her her vineyards,
    and make the Valley of Achor a door of hope.
There she shall respond as in the days of her youth,
    as at the time when she came out of the land of
        Egypt.
16 On that day, says the LORD, you will call me, "My husband,"
and no longer will you call me, "My Baal." 17 For I will remove the
names of the Baals from her mouth, and they shall be mentioned by
name no more. 18 I will make for you a covenant on that day with
the wild animals, the birds of the air, and the creeping things of the
ground; and I will abolish the bow, the sword, and war from the
land; and I will make you lie down in safety. 19 And I will take you
for my wife forever; I will take you for my wife in righteousness and
in justice, in steadfast love, and in mercy. 20 I will take you for my
wife in faithfulness; and you shall know the LORD.

You Can Keep Your Sacrifices

6:4 What shall I do with you, O Ephraim?
    What shall I do with you, O Judah?
Your love is like a morning cloud,
    like the dew that goes away early.
5 Therefore I have hewn them by the prophets,
    I have killed them by the words of my mouth,
    and my judgment goes forth as the light.

6 For I desire steadfast love and not sacrifice,
    the knowledge of God rather than burnt offerings.

7 But at Adam they transgressed the covenant;
    there they dealt faithlessly with me.
8 Gilead is a city of evildoers,
    tracked with blood.
9 As robbers lie in wait for someone,
    so the priests are banded together;
they murder on the road to Shechem,
    they commit a monstrous crime. . . .

11 For you also, O Judah, a harvest is appointed.

The Company You Keep

7:8 Ephraim mixes himself with the peoples;
    Ephraim is a cake not turned. . . .

11 Ephraim has become like a dove,
    silly and without sense;
    they call upon Egypt, they go to Assyria.
12 As they go, I will cast my net over them;
    I will bring them down like birds of the air;
    I will discipline them according to the report made
        to their assembly.
13 Woe to them, for they have strayed from me!
    Destruction to them, for they have rebelled against me!
I would redeem them,
    but they speak lies against me. . . .

16 They turn to that which does not profit;
    they have become like a defective bow;
their officials shall fall by the sword
    because of the rage of their tongue.
So much for their babbling in the land of Egypt.

10 minutes
Choose questions according to your interest and time.

1   In 2:14–20, what is God's strategy for getting the people of Israel to return to him?

2   What is it that God truly desires from his people (6:6)?

3   Is Hosea's announcement that "a harvest is appointed" (6:11) for the people of Judah a promise of blessing? Why or why not?

4   What might the metaphors in 7:8, 7:11, and 7:16 suggest about Israel's behavior?

A Guide to the Reading

If participants have not read this section already, read it aloud. Otherwise go on to "Questions for Application."

2:7, 14–20. The first three chapters of Hosea present what is probably his most powerful imagery, comparing the people of Israel to an unfaithful spouse. Hosea makes it very clear that the love between God and Israel is passionate, not only in a romantic sense but as a love that involves duty and obligation—an obligation that Israel has reneged on. Verse 7 tells us that Israel has other lovers, referring to the worship of Canaanite fertility gods—the Baals—by some of the Israelites. Hosea is chiefly concerned with Israel's misplaced trust. Israelite worshippers of Baal were, in essence, attributing their well-being to a god other than the God of Israel. What is astonishing here is God's willingness to take Israel back. We find God devising strategies for a "second honeymoon." He talks about alluring Israel into the desert, the place where Israel first made her pledge of love and fidelity to God, who brought her out of slavery and into freedom (Exodus 24:3–8). When Hosea says that Israel shall refer to God as "My husband" and no longer call him "My Baal" (2:16), he is drawing attention to the involvement of Israel in the cult of Baal. As we read on, it will become clear that one of the reasons Hosea rejects idolatry is that it brings with it values that are contrary to the covenant with the God of Israel, contrary to "righteousness and . . . justice . . . steadfast love . . . and . . . mercy" (2:19). Worshipping false gods undermines proper ethical and moral behavior.

      6:4–9, 11. Like an exasperated parent, God is expressing frustration over his children Ephraim and Judah—the two dominant tribes of the Israelites that here represent all twelve tribes. God is lamenting out loud, showing his compassionate, loving concern for his children, whose love evaporates as quickly and easily as the morning dew. At this point, Hosea presents one of God's most powerful messages, insisting that God desires steadfast love and not sacrifices. Hosea makes it clear, once again, that ethical behavior is at the heart of the covenant. Ritual sacrifices were meant to be external expressions of one's adoration of God and obedience to God's law of love for one's neighbor. Without love and knowledge of God, such sacrifices become hollow and empty. When one's conduct contradicts the requirements of the covenant—as is happening in the lives of the religious leaders (6:7–9; see also 7:1–3)—sacrifices become outright hypocrisy. Hosea makes it clear that God is not interested in ritual expressions of loyalty to him unless they reflect an inner conversion and a change in relating to other people.

In 6:11, we learn that a harvest awaits the people of Israel. These words are not at all comforting. At harvesttime, one reaps what one has sown. God's people have sown the seeds of immorality, committing violent crimes (6:8–9). The warning of an imminent harvest is another way of saying "you're gonna get yours."

7:8, 11–13, 16. Hosea reaches back into his bag of metaphors for two more powerful images. First, in 7:8, he compares Israel to a cake that is unturned, meaning not fully baked. If you've ever grilled a burger at an outdoor barbecue, you know full well that if you leave a patty unturned, it gets burned on one side while the other side remains raw—in other words, useless. Here, Hosea is indicting Israel for its half-baked policies and practices. He has already rebuked them for social policies that result in a few people being rich while most are poor, and for religious practices that are divorced from ethical and moral behavior. Here he deals with foreign policy that trusts in shaky alliances instead of trusting in God. In 7:11, Hosea compares Israel to a silly, senseless dove fluttering back and forth with no sense of direction between her neighbors Egypt and Assyria, both of whom presented a threat to Israel's very existence. Such a dove is very gullible and easily trapped—an apt metaphor for the people of Israel, who will soon find themselves trapped by Assyria. Hosea compares Israel to "a defective bow" (7:16). Because of her ill-conceived pursuit of alliances with Egypt and Assyria and her neglect of the covenant, Israel will lose her power. God reminds the people of Israel that he alone is their strength. As a result of their sin, they will be the subjects of ridicule when they once again find themselves strangers in a strange land.

Questions for Application

40 minutes
Choose questions according to your interest and time.

1 What does it mean for you (and what difference does it make for you) to know that God's love is passionate and that God is always forgiving?

2 How is the issue of forgiveness tied to justice? How can God's loving forgiveness help you to live more justly?

3 Hosea tells us in 2:14 that God intends to allure Israel into the desert to renew their relationship. Where would God invite you to go to renew your relationship with him? How is spiritual renewal tied to working for justice?

4 In response to God's loving invitation, what personal behaviors do you feel led to change in order to contribute to a more just society?

5 Hosea characterizes God's love for Israel as unconditional. How is God's love for Israel a model for how we are to behave toward our neighbors? What does it mean, in practical terms, to love others unconditionally?

6 Where is the message of forgiveness and hope most needed today so that justice may prevail? What are the obstacles to the message's being heard? Where are Christians working to minister God's love to the oppressed and suffering? How is Christian service different from service work performed by secular humanitarian organizations?

7 Idolatry involves false values. What false values—that is, values contrary to the gospel—are most prevalent in society today? What are you tempted to find fulfillment in instead of in God?

8 In what ways are we as a society silly and senseless, like the dove that Israel was compared to? In what ways do we seek security in misplaced alliances? To whom or what are we, as a society, allying ourselves? Where or how do you sometimes seek security, aside from God?

In the Bible we ponder the principal events of the history of salvation. We study these events in their historical reality, and in them we meet God.

Sofia Cavalletti, *History's Golden Thread: The History of Salvation*

Approach to Prayer

15 minutes
Use this approach—or create your own!

♦ Ask someone to read aloud the words of Clement of Alexandria:

For to everyone who has turned to God in truth and with a whole heart, the doors are open, and the thrice-glad Father receives his truly repentant child. And true repentance is to be no longer bound in the same sins for which he denounced . . . himself, but to eradicate them completely from the soul. For on their uprooting, God takes up his abode again in you.

Take a moment of silence for each person to consider what sins against justice need to be uprooted in his or her own life. Then invite the group to offer petitions for those in the world who are suffering oppression and injustice, as well as for the transformation of those who are the oppressors.

Saints in the Making

Insisting on the Just Treatment of Workers

This section is a supplement for individual reading.

In the 1980s, frustrated workers in Poland looked to a modern-day prophet named Lech Walesa to unite them in solidarity against a regime that refused to grant them freedom and dignity. In the winter of 1970, when a conflict between shipyard workers and the Communist government erupted, Walesa, an electrician, emerged as a leader of the movement. Over the next decade, Walesa continued to struggle for the rights of workers. In late summer of 1980, Walesa led the strike in the Gdańsk shipyard, giving rise to a number of strikes throughout much of the country. All across Poland, Walesa was seen as the leader of what came to be known as the Solidarity movement. Communist authorities eventually were forced to negotiate with Walesa, resulting in an agreement that gave the workers the right to strike as well as to form an independent union. Catholic officials gave their support to the movement, as exemplified by Pope John Paul II, who warmly received Walesa at the Vatican in January of 1981.

However, in December 1981, General Wojciech Jaruzelski, the leader of Poland's Communist regime, suspended Solidarity, arrested many of its leaders, and placed Walesa under house arrest. In late 1982, Walesa was released and allowed to return to the Gdańsk shipyards. Although kept under close watch, he continued to stay in contact with underground Solidarity. When it was announced in October 1983 that Walesa had been awarded the Nobel Peace Prize, the underground movement felt emboldened. As economic conditions continued to deteriorate, the Jaruzelski government dropped dramatically in popularity. Jaruzelski eventually realized he had no choice but to negotiate with Walesa and Solidarity. As a result, parliamentary elections were held, leading to the establishment of a noncommunist government. Without fear of intervention from a weakened Soviet Union, Walesa, who had become the leader of Solidarity, participated in a number of meetings with a variety of world leaders, even speaking to a joint session of the United States Congress. In December 1990, Lech Walesa was elected president of the Republic of Poland, thus completing his journey from shipyard electrician to president of a free country—a journey that was propelled by his insistence on the just treatment of workers.

FINDING OUR WAY HOME

Questions to Begin

15 minutes
Use a question or two to get warmed up for the reading.

---

1 Recall a time when a teacher or a parent told you that a punishment would be "for your own good." Did it turn out that way?

---

2 When in your life has something good come out of a bad experience?

5 minutes
Read the passage aloud. Let individuals take turns reading sections.

The Reading: Hosea 10:12–14; 11:1–4, 8–9; 14:1–5, 7, 9

The Time Is Now

10:12 Sow for yourselves righteousness;
    reap steadfast love;
    break up your fallow ground;
  for it is time to seek the LORD,
    that he may come and rain righteousness upon you.
13 You have plowed wickedness,
    you have reaped injustice,
    you have eaten the fruit of lies.
  Because you have trusted in your power
    and in the multitude of your warriors,
14 therefore the tumult of war shall rise against your people,
    and all your fortresses shall be destroyed. . . .

I Could Never Stop Loving You

11:1 When Israel was a child, I loved him,
    and out of Egypt I called my son.
2 The more I called them,
    the more they went from me;
  they kept sacrificing to the Baals,
    and offering incense to idols.
3 Yet it was I who taught Ephraim to walk,
    I took them up in my arms;
    but they did not know that I healed them.
4 I led them with cords of human kindness,
    with bands of love.
  I was to them like those
    who lift infants to their cheeks.
  I bent down to them and fed them. . . .

8 How can I give you up, Ephraim?
    How can I hand you over, O Israel? . . .
  My heart recoils within me;
    my compassion grows warm and tender.

 ⁹ I will not execute my fierce anger;
　　I will not again destroy Ephraim;
　for I am God and no mortal,
　　the Holy One in your midst,
　　and I will not come in wrath.

A Reason to Hope

14:1 Return, O Israel, to the Lord your God,
　　for you have stumbled because of your iniquity.
　² Take words with you
　　and return to the Lord;
　say to him,
　　"Take away all guilt;
　accept that which is good,
　　and we will offer
　　the fruit of our lips.
　³ Assyria shall not save us;
　　we will not ride upon horses;
　we will say no more, 'Our God,'
　　to the work of our hands.
　In you the orphan finds mercy."

　⁴ I will heal their disloyalty;
　　I will love them freely,
　　for my anger has turned from them.
　⁵ I will be like the dew to Israel;
　　he shall blossom like the lily,
　　he shall strike root like the forests of Lebanon. . . .
　⁷ They shall again live beneath my shadow,
　　they shall flourish as a garden;
　they shall blossom like the vine,
　　their fragrance shall be like the wine of Lebanon. . . .

　⁹ Those who are wise understand these things;
　　those who are discerning know them.
　For the ways of the Lord are right,
　　and the upright walk in them,
　　but transgressors stumble in them.

10 minutes
Choose questions according to your interest and time.

1 In 10:12–13, what farming images does Hosea use? Taking the images one by one, what point is he making through each of them?

2 From the rest of this week's reading, what kind of "wickedness" (10:13) do the people of Israel seem to have planted?

3 Hosea says that those who remain faithful to the covenant will "reap steadfast love" (10:12). What does it mean to experience God's steadfast love? What experience of another person's love has helped you understand God's steadfast love?

4 Where does Hosea include messages of hope along with his gloom and doom? What is the purpose of including these messages?

5 What image in these passages would you consider to be the most tender? What message does it communicate?

6 On what kind of a note does the message of Hosea end?

A Guide to the Reading

If participants have not read this section already, read it aloud. Otherwise go on to "Questions for Application."

10:12–14. Up to this point, we have focused on Hosea's message of doom. However, in 10:12, we begin to see a glimmer of hope. Hosea offers the people of Israel an alternative, namely, sowing seeds of righteousness that will produce a harvest of steadfast love. The challenge for Hosea's listeners and for readers of all generations is to determine what it means, in practical terms, to sow seeds of righteousness. The image of breaking up fallow ground is one of great possibility, since this is something that the farmer does in anticipation of sowing seeds for the upcoming growing season.

No sooner does Hosea offer these images of hope, however, than he returns to his indictment. Using the harvest image, he reminds the people of Israel that they have been harvesting the wrong crop, namely, wickedness, injustice, and dishonesty. None of these are the fruit of a covenant relationship with God. Hosea also points out that, instead of trusting in God, Israel has trusted in herself and in her own power. Hosea bluntly insists that this will be her downfall, saying, in essence, that the sword she has lived by will be the instrument of her destruction.

11:1–4, 8–9. The opening verses of this chapter employ some of the most tender imagery in the Bible. Moving away from the imagery of a marriage torn by adultery, Hosea now uses the image of a loving parent and a wayward child. A parent allows a child to make mistakes so that the child can learn from them. But this loving parent is lamenting over a wayward child, recalling what used to be an intimate relationship. The reference to calling this child out of Egypt once again brings to mind the beginning of the relationship between Israel and God that was formed in the desert following the exodus. However, the child, Israel, has strayed from this intimate relationship. In 11:3, Hosea uses an image that is one of his favorites, namely, the image of God as healer. The "cords of human kindness" and the "bands of love" (11:4) bring to mind the kiddie leashes that some parents use today to keep a close watch on children in crowded places.

In 11:8–9, we find God speaking directly to his children with great passion, using rhetorical questions to assure them that they are going to receive a second chance. God has the right to assign total destruction to Israel, but, as a loving parent, God refuses that right in favor of compassion. God explains that such radical compassion is possible because he is God and "no mortal" (11:9).

14:1–5, 7, 9. Like most of the biblical prophets, Hosea ends his prophecy on a hopeful note. The opening lines of this chapter begin with an exhortation to return to God. Hosea, in fact, provides the people of Israel with a script in 14:2–3, telling them the very words they should use to persuade God of their sincerity. An attitude of arrogance and self-reliance is at the very core of idolatry, because idolatry rejects total reliance upon the one and only God in favor of some other source of imagined fulfillment. Thus, Hosea directs the people to say that they will no longer say "'Our God' to the work of" their hands (14:3). Hosea points out that, just as an orphan is totally reliant upon the love of adoptive parents, the people of Israel must recognize their salvation in the compassion of their loving God.

In 14:4, we encounter God's tender response, as God announces his intentions of restoring—healing—his people. Hosea now returns to his bag of metaphors as he compares God to the morning dew, that precious and life-giving moisture that appears each morning, keeping vegetation alive during the dry seasons. In the same way, God promises to bring refreshment to his parched people who, in turn, will blossom like a lily. In 14:6–7, Hosea compares God to a huge tree giving shade in the midst of scorching heat. In this comforting shade, Israel shall flourish. Finally, in 14:9, we can imagine Hosea taking hold of a microphone and standing atop a crate to get everyone's attention as he shouts out that the wise and discerning should be able to grasp his message. This final exhortation is a call to action. God's invitation demands a response—a response grounded in wisdom and justice.

Questions for Application

40 minutes
Choose questions according to your interest and time.

1   Consider Hosea's image of sowing seeds. Give some examples of people addressing social problems in small, hidden ways, where the results took time.

2   What is our society sowing today that is contrary to what God asks of us? What does it mean to sow the seeds of righteousness today? What can you do to sow such seeds?

3   As a prophet, Hosea is in the position of correcting the people of Israel. Are you in a position to correct someone for oppressive behavior? How well do you respond to correction? What kind of loving correction would a parent offer to you in terms of your behavior toward others?

4   Hosea explains that idolatry is saying "Our God" to the work of our hands. In what ways do we lift the work of our own hands to the level of idolatry in today's society?

5   In Hosea, the call to justice is a call to renewal, like bringing nourishment to a parched land. In what ways are injustices causing our society to become parched? What can we do to bring about renewal?

6   In what ways can individuals help to bring about a more just society? What does it mean to help others walk in the way of the Lord? What gifts can you personally put to use in such efforts?

Scripture comes alive most in relationships and in relationship to the tradition of the Church.

Patrick J. Brennan, *Re-Imagining the Parish*

Approach to Prayer

15 minutes
Use this approach—or create your own!

♦ Invite participants to silently
recall a time in their lives when
they strayed from the Lord.
Then invite the group to pray the
Lord's Prayer to our loving
Father and a Hail Mary, asking
our mother for her help in
remaining close to God.

Saints in the Making

Changing the World in Small Ways

This section is a supplement for individual reading.

When we think of people committed to working for justice, we may think of those who engage in dramatic and extraordinary actions. The fact is, however, that we can work to make the world a more just place in small, everyday ways. Consider the following examples:

♦ John received permission to sell snacks in the company kitchen. He purchases snacks at low prices and sells them to coworkers for a small markup, donating the profits to a charity.

♦ When Latonya takes her teenage boys shopping for gym shoes, she explains to them why she will not spend exorbitant amounts of money on shoes that are made by young children who work in harsh conditions and get paid almost nothing.

♦ Gail is an eighth-grade catechist who helps to arrange field trips each year to the local soup kitchen, where students serve meals to those who are less fortunate.

♦ Veronica, Susan, and Alice are retired senior citizens who, with the support of the parish pastoral associate, began offering a "Mom's Morning Out" at their parish so that the young moms could drop their little ones off with "a bunch of grandmas" and use the time to socialize, shop, or just take a nap.

♦ Mike goes through his drawers and closet several times each year to find clothes to donate to the St. Vincent De Paul Center to help people in need.

♦ When Miguel and Velma took their eighteen-year-old son, Ernesto, to register to vote, they explained to him that he should vote to support efforts that respect the needs of the poor and vulnerable and to oppose anything that might deprive them of their basic needs and dignity.

♦ Glenn regularly checks the Red Cross Web site to see where there are people around the world in need of emergency help.

♦ Martha signed up for the village recycling plan to help conserve the world's resources, to care for God's creation, and to ensure abundance for generations to come.

The list could go on. None of these people will ever become famous or be canonized as a saint. They are ordinary people like us, who can and do make the world a more just place to live.

Week 5

THE CHOICE IS YOURS

Questions to Begin

15 minutes
Use a question or two to get warmed up for the reading.

---

1 What choices did you make today in the first hour after you awakened?

---

2 Describe yourself as a decision maker: Do you tend to make quick decisions, or do you take your time deliberating?

Opening the Bible

5 minutes
Read the passage aloud. Let individuals take turns reading sections.

The Reading: Amos 5:6–7, 11–12, 14–15, 18–24; 9:11–15

It's Your Choice

> 5:6 Seek the LORD and live,
>> or he will break out against the house of Joseph like fire,
>> and it will devour Bethel, with no one to quench it.
> 7 Ah, you that turn justice to wormwood,
>> and bring righteousness to the ground! . . .
>
> 11 Therefore because you trample on the poor
>> and take from them levies of grain,
> you have built houses of hewn stone,
>> but you shall not live in them;
> you have planted pleasant vineyards,
>> but you shall not drink their wine.
> 12 . . . you who afflict the righteous, who take a bribe,
>> and push aside the needy in the gate. . . .
>
> 14 Seek good and not evil,
>> that you may live;
> and so the LORD, the God of hosts, will be with you,
>> just as you have said.
> 15 Hate evil and love good,
>> and establish justice in the gate;
> it may be that the LORD, the God of hosts,
>> will be gracious to the remnant of Joseph. . . .

The Day Is Coming

> 18 Alas for you who desire the day of the LORD!
>> Why do you want the day of the LORD?
> It is darkness, not light;
> 19   as if someone fled from a lion,
>> and was met by a bear;
> or went into the house and rested a hand against the wall,
>> and was bitten by a snake.
> 20 Is not the day of the LORD darkness, not light,
>> and gloom with no brightness in it?

21 I hate, I despise your festivals,
    and I take no delight in your solemn assemblies.
22 Even though you offer me your burnt offerings and
        grain offerings,
    I will not accept them;
  and the offerings of well-being of your fatted animals
    I will not look upon.
23 Take away from me the noise of your songs;
    I will not listen to the melody of your harps.
24 But let justice roll down like waters,
    and righteousness like an ever-flowing stream.

Everything's Going to Be All Right

9:11 On that day I will raise up
    the booth of David that is fallen,
  and repair its breaches,
    and raise up its ruins,
    and rebuild it as in the days of old;
12 in order that they may possess the remnant of Edom
    and all the nations who are called by my name,
    says the LORD who does this.

13 The time is surely coming, says the LORD,
    when the one who plows shall overtake the one who
        reaps,
    and the treader of grapes the one who sows the seed;
  the mountains shall drip sweet wine,
    and all the hills shall flow with it.
14 I will restore the fortunes of my people Israel,
    and they shall rebuild the ruined cities and inhabit
        them;
  they shall plant vineyards and drink their wine,
    and they shall make gardens and eat their fruit.
15 I will plant them upon their land,
    and they shall never again be plucked up
    out of the land that I have given them,
               says the LORD your God.

10 minutes
Choose questions according to your interest and time.

1 From other statements that Amos makes in this week's reading, what does he mean by the words "seek the Lord and live" (5:6)?

2 What types of injustices does Amos describe in 5:11–12? How do these compare with injustices that have been identified by Micah and Hosea (especially Micah 2:2; 3:2–3, 11 and Hosea 6:7–9; 10:12–14)? Putting together the descriptions of the three prophets, what picture do you get of Israelite society?

3 What choices does God lay before the people of Israel in 5:14–15?

4 Having read 5:18–20, how would you describe the "day of the Lord" to someone?

5 What connection do you see between worship and justice from 5:21–24?

6 How does the tone of 9:11–15 compare with that of the other excerpts from Amos in this week's reading and in the readings from Week 1?

A Guide to the Reading

If participants have not read this section already, read it aloud. Otherwise go on to "Questions for Application."

5:6–7, 11–12, 14–15. Amos makes it very clear that the people of Israel face a choice that has either life-giving or destructive consequences. When Amos speaks of making the choice to "live" (5:6), he is speaking about much more than mere survival or existence. Rather, to live is to prosper, to have a full and vital life. This fullness of life can be found only by seeking the Lord.

Amos once again points out blatant social injustices in Israel, most notably, economic practices that exploit the poor. Verse 11 points to the practice of the wealthy building large, luxurious homes while the poor do not have enough to eat.

In 5:14–15, Amos makes it clear that by choosing good over evil, Israel will have what it yearns for more than anything— God in their midst. Amos asserts that to seek God and to love good are more than just feelings or attitudes; they are decisions to be followed by actions. Verse 15 states that justice must be established at the gate of Israel. Traditionally, the gate of a city was the place where those with a complaint could find the elders of the community to pass judgment. Amos was not talking about establishing justice at a physical location but within the judicial institutions of Israel. Moreover, he insists that justice should not only be accessible for all the people of Israel but should also be the foundation for every aspect of their lives. The call in 5:15, "establish justice," may also be translated "produce justice" or "let justice prevail"—a bold imperative that articulates God's priorities for our lives.

5:18–24. In 5:18, we encounter the concept of the "day of the Lord"—a concept that expressed Israel's belief that God would burst into their midst to fulfill the promise he had made to Abraham by defeating his enemies. In his own inimitable style, Amos pops this bubble of complacency, totally reversing Israel's expectations: for them, the day of the Lord will be not a day of victory but a day of wrath. Verse 19 uses language similar to our contemporary image of jumping from the frying pan into the fire as another way of saying, "If you think things are bad now, just wait until the day of the Lord!" God's presence will expose the evils being committed by his people and will bring about the painful consequences that result from their actions.

In 5:21–24, Amos speaks not about what is wrong with the way the people worship but about what is wrong with the worshippers. God is not interested in receiving ritual sacrifices from people who refuse to live in an ethical manner. In one of the most famous verses of the Bible, God says, "Let justice roll down like waters, and righteousness like an ever-flowing stream" (5:24). In other words, justice and righteousness are prerequisites for worship.

9:11–15. Although Amos follows the prophetic tradition of ending on an upbeat note with a message of hope, the consequences of the sinful behavior of the people of Israel are unavoidable. The restoration of the people of Israel will occur only after the destruction of the kingdom of Israel.

Amos hints at a revival of the Davidic kingdom (9:11). It is important to note that the kingship that Amos has in mind is the type that takes responsibility for justice in society. Amos is speaking here about kingship that aims at good government, not at conquest and domination. With images of repairing and rebuilding, Amos lets it be known that the destruction of Israel will serve a purpose; namely, it will give the people an opportunity to refocus on the heart of the covenant, which is love of God and neighbor. Amos indicates that the restoration of Israel will be the work of the Lord. All of this uplifting talk does not refute Amos's earlier warnings. Rather, it completes the story, providing those who face the daunting task of reforming and rebuilding their lives with a broad perspective that includes hope, consolation, and mercy.

Questions for Application

40 minutes
Choose questions according to your interest and time.

1 What does it mean to you to "seek the Lord" (5:6)?

2 What does it mean, in practical terms, to love good and hate evil? What kinds of actions flow from this basic choice?

3 What would change in your life if you were to let justice be the basis of all of your actions?

4 Where are the "gates" of our society—those places where justice needs to prevail?

5 What injustices would the "day of the Lord" (5:18–20)—the realization of God's presence in our midst—expose in today's world?

6 What choices does our society face that will result in either life-giving or destructive consequences?

7 What parts of the Mass speak most directly to you about living in an ethical manner?

If we are rigidly convinced of a single interpretation, we are not able to hear something new or unexpected and . . . we may not be able to receive new information and insights that challenge the way we see things. We may not be open to change.

Joye Gros, *Theological Reflection: Connecting Faith and Life*

Approach to Prayer

15 minutes
Use this approach—or create your own!

♦ Invite the participants to share petitions out loud for those who are victims of injustice. After each petition, invite all to respond: "Lord, let justice prevail." After each participant has had an opportunity to share their petition, conclude by having one of the participants read the following words of St. Ambrose:

Let us hurry to him in whom is that highest good, since he is goodness itself. He is the patience of Israel calling you to repentance, so you will not come to judgment but may receive the remission of sins. He is the one of whom the prophet Amos cries, "Seek good" (5:14). He is the highest good . . . of whose fullness we have all received and in whom we have been filled, as the evangelist says (John 1:16).

Conclude by praying the Lord's Prayer together.

A Living Tradition

Justice and Stewardship

This section is a supplement for individual reading.

The prophets' call to establish a more just society challenges us to live as caretakers of God's gifts and to use them wisely for the good of all. In 1986, the U.S. Catholic Bishops addressed this issue in their pastoral letter *Economic Justice for All.*

Economic life raises important social and moral questions for each of us and for the society as a whole. Like family life, economic life is one of the chief areas where we live out our faith, love our neighbor, confront temptation, fulfill God's creative design, and achieve holiness. Our economic activity in factory, field, office, or shop feeds our families—or feeds our anxieties. It exercises our talents—or wastes them. It raises our hopes—or crushes them. It brings us into cooperation with others—or sets us at odds. The Second Vatican Council instructs us "to preach the message of Christ in such a way that the light of the Gospel will shine on all activities of the faithful" (Pastoral Constitution on the Church in the Modern World, section 43). In this case, we are trying to look at economic life through the eyes of faith, applying traditional church teaching to the U.S. economy. . . .

As Catholics, we are heirs of a long tradition of thought and action on the moral dimensions of economic activity. The life and words of Jesus and the teaching of his Church call us to serve those in need and to work actively for social and economic justice. As a community of believers, we know that our faith is tested by the quality of justice among us, that we can best measure our life together by how the poor and the vulnerable are treated. This is not a new concern for us. It is as old as the Hebrew prophets, as compelling as the Sermon on the Mount, and as current as the powerful voice of Pope John Paul II defending the dignity of the human person.

KEEPING HOPE ALIVE

Questions to Begin

15 minutes
Use a question or two to get warmed up for the reading.

1 What do you find yourself wishing for more than anything else?

2 Think of someone you know who has a great imagination. How do they put their imagination to work?

5 minutes
*Read the passage aloud. Let individuals take turns reading
sections.*

The Reading: Micah 4:1–3, 6–7; 5:2–5; 6:8; 7:18–20

Better Days Are Coming

4:1 In days to come
    the mountain of the LORD's house
shall be established as the highest of the mountains,
    and shall be raised up above the hills.
Peoples shall stream to it,
2   and many nations shall come and say:
"Come, let us go up to the mountain of the LORD,
    to the house of the God of Jacob;
that he may teach us his ways
    and that we may walk in his paths."
For out of Zion shall go forth instruction,
    and the word of the LORD from Jerusalem.
3 He shall judge between many peoples,
    and shall arbitrate between strong nations far away;
they shall beat their swords into plowshares,
    and their spears into pruning hooks;
nation shall not lift up sword against nation,
    neither shall they learn war any more. . . .

6 In that day, says the LORD,
    I will assemble the lame
and gather those who have been driven away,
    and those whom I have afflicted.
7 The lame I will make the remnant,
    and those who were cast off, a strong nation;
and the LORD will reign over them in Mount Zion
    now and forevermore.

The Fulfillment of a Promise

5:2 But you, O Bethlehem of Ephrathah,
    who are one of the little clans of Judah,
from you shall come forth for me
    one who is to rule in Israel,

whose origin is from of old,
  from ancient days.
³ Therefore he shall give them up until the time
  when she who is in labor has brought forth;
then the rest of his kindred shall return
  to the people of Israel.
⁴ And he shall stand and feed his flock in the strength of
      the Lord,
  in the majesty of the name of the Lord his God.
And they shall live secure, for now he shall be great
  to the ends of the earth;
⁵ and he shall be the one of peace.

The Heart of the Message

⁶:⁸ He has told you, O mortal, what is good;
  and what does the Lord require of you
but to do justice, and to love kindness,
  and to walk humbly with your God?

God's Compassion and Steadfast Love

⁷:¹⁸ Who is a God like you, pardoning iniquity
  and passing over the transgression
  of the remnant of your possession?
He does not retain his anger forever,
  because he delights in showing clemency.
¹⁹ He will again have compassion upon us;
  he will tread our iniquities under foot.
You will cast all our sins
  into the depths of the sea.
²⁰ You will show faithfulness to Jacob
  and unswerving loyalty to Abraham,
as you have sworn to our ancestors
  from the days of old.

10 minutes
Choose questions according to your interest and time.

1 How does Micah use imagination as a tool for building a vision for the future in 4:1–7?

2 What does the image of "the mountain of the Lord's house" (4:1) suggest to you? What would it mean to Micah's listeners to be told that people from many nations would come streaming to the mountain of the Lord?

3 In 4:3, what does it mean to beat "swords into plowshares" and "spears into pruning hooks"?

4 From what is said in 5:2, why might Bethlehem be considered an unlikely location from which the Messiah would emerge? What does this say about the way God fulfills his plans?

5 Which of God's qualities described in 7:18–20 strikes you as most powerful or compelling? Why?

A Guide to the Reading

If participants have not read this section already, read it aloud. Otherwise go on to "Questions for Application."

4:1–3, 6–7. The very first words of chapter 4—"in days to come"—point toward a distant future. This gives us a clue that Micah is speaking in idealized terms here, encouraging the people who find themselves mired in despair to use their imaginations as a vehicle toward reestablishing hope. This longed-for and promised age to come, often referred to as the messianic age, would fulfill God's promise to bring an end to oppression and a return of what was lost, namely, a world in which God reigns. Anyone who knows the geography of the area surrounding Jerusalem knows that the "mountain of the Lord's house" (4:1)—the temple—is nowhere near the highest mountain in the area. Micah is speaking not of physical height here but of status. In other words, after a period of humiliation, Israel will be restored to her favored status with God. Micah speaks of an age of peace in which people of all nations will stream up toward Jerusalem while, at the same moment, God's instruction will be flowing down.

Verse 3 includes one of the most famous prophetic passages in the Bible—the idea of beating "swords into plowshares" and "spears into pruning hooks." Basically, Micah is indicating that God will impose justice on the earth, bringing an end to worldly powers that use violence to attain their ends. The instruments of war will no longer be needed for defense and can be transformed into tools for the growth and nourishment of all people. In 4:6–7, Micah promises that the lame, the afflicted, and the outcasts—and even those who have been made to suffer punishment for their injustices—will experience God's rich mercy and compassion.

5:2–5. Micah continues with his references to a messianic age when God's promises will be fulfilled and Israel's hopes achieved. One hope associated with these expectations was that the messiah would be a ruler descended from David. Since David was born in Bethlehem, the promise of the messiah's birth taking place in David's hometown would be seen as a promise that God would continue to move toward this fulfillment. Thus, despite the people's sins, God will continue his covenant with them. The message is clear: God does not break his promises even when it appears as though he has forgotten them. Bethlehem is called "one of the little clans" (5:2). Indeed, it was a small place. God reveals that when he does something great, his action does not match human expectations or standards.

Verse 3 refers to "she who is in labor." For the people of Micah's time, this was less a description of a particular person than an indication that before this age of joy there would be a period of waiting, marked by labor pains—pains of anticipation. Micah is encouraging the people of Israel not to lose heart.

This new leader—the messiah—is referred to as one who will feed his flock, invoking the image of a shepherd. The source of the shepherd's strength, protection, and peace will be the Lord.

6:8. This verse stands by itself as one of the greatest statements of God's expectations for us. It takes us to the very heart of the prophets' calls to us.

7:18–20. This section of Micah most likely dates from the time after the exile in Babylon, when the people of Israel are returning to find their homeland in ruins. As bad as things are for the people of Israel, Micah sees fit to end on a note of hope. Verse 18 asks the powerful rhetorical question "Who is a God like you?"—a question that echoes the name of the prophet, for in Hebrew, *Micah* is a short form of "Who is like God?" In fact, there is no one who can compare with him. God surpasses everyone else in his capacity for being forgiving, compassionate, faithful, and loyal, for not holding anger, and for delighting in mercy. Each of these qualities of God is a quality that those who are in covenant with God are to imitate in their relationships with one another. It is only by remaining faithful to the covenant tradition of practicing compassion, mercy, and justice that the people of Israel can look hopefully to the future. In the end, Micah tells the people of Israel that when the damage of their injustices has run its course, God's inner nature will shine through.

Questions for Application

40 minutes
Choose questions according to your interest and time.

1 What purpose does it serve to speak in idealized terms when people are in despair? What role does imagination play when speaking to people who have lost hope?

2 How can you spread a message of hope in your daily living?

3 What is God's proper place in society? What would it mean in practical terms to restore God to his proper place in society? What does it mean to place God first in a society where church and state are separated?

4 Is it possible for nations to turn "swords into plowshares" and "spears into pruning hooks" (4:3)? What would it look like in practical terms?

5 Just as God brought about the Messiah from an unexpected place called Bethlehem, how has he acted in surprising and unexpected ways in your life?

6 In 7:18–20, Micah describes the qualities of God. What qualities of God are most needed in society today, with regard to family life, social issues, the dignity of human life, the economy, and the environment?

7 What quality do you most need to incorporate into your own life in order to be more like God as he is described in 7:18–20?

8 Micah asserts that God will remain true to his promise to restore Israel to her former status. To the people of Israel, this meant a return to the land they claimed as theirs. How do we interpret God's promise for society today? What does it mean for God to restore us to a former status? How is God keeping his promise?

Our encounters with God will make a difference in us that may not be immediately perceptible. For one thing, in time we will reflect the Word that we have taken into our hearts. We will be more Christlike, living with the mind and heart of Christ. In this way we will resemble Mary, the listening virgin, and bring forth Christ into the world.

Mary Kathleen Glavich, *The Bible Way to Prayer*

Approach to Prayer

15 minutes
Use this approach—or create your own!

♦ Invite the participants to share their favorite passage on justice from the readings of the past six weeks. Then, invite participants to renew their baptismal commitments to let justice prevail by responding "I do" to each of the following.

Leader:
❑ Do you reject Satan?
❑ And all his works?
❑ And all his empty promises?
❑ Do you believe in God, the Father almighty, Creator of heaven and earth?
❑ Do you believe in Jesus Christ, His only Son, our Lord, Who was born of the Virgin Mary, was crucified, died, and was buried, rose from the dead, and is now seated at the right hand of the Father?
❑ Do you believe in the Holy Spirit, the holy Catholic Church, the communion of saints, the forgiveness of sins, the resurrection of the body, and life everlasting?

This is our faith. This is the faith of the Church. We are proud to profess it, in Christ Jesus our Lord. Amen.

Saints in the Making

A Good Start

This section is a supplement for individual reading.

In the movie *Philadelphia,* in which Denzel Washington and Tom Hanks star as lawyers, a character tells the following joke: "What do you call a thousand lawyers chained together at the bottom of the ocean? . . . A good start."

While lawyers often get a bad rap, here is a story about two lawyers who have dedicated their lives to making sure that the poor of our society have access to the justice system. For over twenty-five years, they have been the driving forces behind the Chicago Legal Clinic.

In the early 1980s, the blue-collar community of South Chicago saw a number of its steel mills closed down, resulting in a 35 percent unemployment rate. A young associate pastor in the area, the Reverend Thomas J. Paprocki (my brother), realized that many of the people coming to him for guidance were in need of not only spiritual assistance but also legal and economic assistance. To better minister to the people of the community, he received permission from the archbishop to attend law school. It was at the DePaul University College of Law that he met Edward Grossman. The two shared their dreams of committing their talents to the assistance of those who normally do not have access to the justice system. Following their graduation and acceptance to the bar, they founded the South Chicago Legal Clinic in a very small storefront office furnished with only a table and a few chairs. Since its founding, the clinic's mission has reflected their commitment: "to identify legal needs and provide community-based quality legal services and education to the underserved and disadvantaged in the Chicago area, thereby promoting justice through greater access to the legal system."

By 2005, the Chicago Legal Clinic had grown to serve over 100,000 clients, operating out of four neighborhood offices and a downtown office, employing a staff of twenty-eight and working with numerous interns and volunteers, as well as a panel of over two hundred pro bono attorneys. Father Paprocki has become an auxiliary bishop of the Archdiocese of Chicago while retaining his position as president of the Chicago Legal Clinic. Edward Grossman continues to serve as the executive director of the clinic, overseeing its day-to-day business.

What do you call two lawyers working to make the justice system accessible to the poor and disadvantaged? A good start.

The Church Is Not a Non-Prophet Organization

Today, as much as in biblical times, the world needs prophets to speak God's truth and to challenge people to live in justice and righteousness. As baptized members of the Church, we have a share in Jesus' prophetic ministry. So just what is a prophet, and what does a prophet do? In simple terms, a prophet is one who

- clearly and boldly speaks God's word
- bears witness to God's saving presence
- speaks on behalf of the oppressed
- evangelizes and catechizes
- brings hope to those in despair
- challenges people and institutions to be faithful to the weak and to those in need
- fearlessly speaks about injustice

In biblical terms, prophets are those people who speak words revealed to them by God. In order to be an effective channel of communication between God and God's people, a prophet must have an intimate connection with God. Filled with passion for God's word, prophets are compelled to speak out, even when doing so threatens their own comfort and security, and even their own existence. Prophets in the biblical tradition do not make wild, generalized predictions of doom. Rather, they speak concretely to specific times, places, and circumstances, bringing people's attention to crises that need to be addressed for the well-being of all. In an attempt to lead others to see reality more truly, prophets use creative approaches aimed at disrupting people's perceptions of reality. To carry out this task, prophets must be people of great imagination.

Imagination, unfortunately, can be viewed negatively. We often use the term *wild imagination* to describe someone who is out of touch with reality. In truth, people with great imaginations may be more in touch with reality than those who are less imaginative. Our imaginations help us see beyond present realities to the realm of possibility. As people of great imagination, prophets are not only acutely aware of what is wrong in society but also have the capacity to see how it might be set right. With this great imagination, prophets are capable of lifting people beyond themselves and of inspiring hope. Even when pointing out ills that need to be corrected, prophets do so out of a firm belief that things can and will be better for people on all sides of the issue.

Biblical prophets proclaimed God's word at great personal cost. In our daily lives, however, we are not called to face the same hazards that the biblical prophets did. Although we still face a personal cost for proclaiming God's word, it is crucial for us to know that people are, indeed, looking for prophecy. Likewise, although we may learn from the strategies of the biblical prophets, we are most likely called to do our prophetic work in less dramatic but no less effective manners, practicing humility and compassion as we call others to transformation. We may not think of ourselves as prophets, because we tend to think that prophets must be fiery orators. However, working for truth and justice can be practiced very quietly, even without words.

To be a prophet in today's world is to be someone with eyes wide open so as to see through lies, shams, and pretenses. To be a prophet in today's world is to practice the virtue of courage—standing up for what you believe in, even when it means going against the status quo. To be a prophet means to be able to embrace the truth, the one and only thing that ultimately will set us free. As disciples of Jesus Christ, we are committed to the one who refers to himself as "the way, and the truth, and the life" (John 14:6).

In baptism, we were anointed with oil, and the following words were addressed to us:

God the Father of our Lord Jesus Christ . . . now anoints you with the chrism of salvation. As Christ was anointed *priest*, *prophet*, and *king*, so may you live always as a member of his body, sharing everlasting life.

Notice the word *prophet.* Sharing in the prophetic ministry of Jesus is not an option. It is an obligation for anyone who calls himself or herself a Christian.

Suggestions for Bible Discussion Groups

Like a camping trip, a Bible discussion group works best if you agree on where you're going and how you intend to get there. Many groups use their first meeting to talk over such questions. Here is a checklist of issues, with bits of advice from people who have experience in Bible discussions. (A planning discussion will go more smoothly if the leaders have thought through the following issues beforehand.)

Agree on your purpose. Are you getting together to gain wisdom and direction for your lives? to finally get acquainted with the Bible? to support one another in following Christ? to encourage those who are exploring—or reexploring—the Church? for other reasons?

Agree on attitudes. For example: "We're all beginners here." "We're here to help one another understand and respond to God's word." "We're not here to offer counseling or direction to one another." "We want to read Scripture prayerfully." What do *you* wish to emphasize? Make it explicit!

Agree on ground rules. Barbara J. Fleischer, in her useful book *Facilitating for Growth,* recommends that a group clearly state its approach to the following:

- *Preparation.* Do we agree to read the material and prepare answers to the questions before each meeting?
- *Attendance.* What kind of priority will we give to our meetings?
- *Self-revelation.* Are we willing to help the others in the group gradually get to know us—our weaknesses as well as our strengths, our needs as well as our gifts?
- *Listening.* Will we commit ourselves to listen to one another?
- *Confidentiality.* Will we keep everything that is shared *with* the group *in* the group?
- *Discretion.* Will we refrain from sharing about the faults and sins of people who are not in the group?
- *Encouragement and support.* Will we give as well as receive?
- *Participation.* Will we give each person the time and opportunity to make a contribution?

You could probably take a pen and draw a circle around *listening* and *confidentiality*. Those two points are especially important.

The following items could be added to Fleischer's list:

♦ *Relationship with parish.* Is our group part of the adult faith-formation program? independent but operating with the express approval of the pastor? not a parish-based group?

♦ *New members.* Will we let new members join us once we have begun the six weeks of discussions?

Agree on housekeeping.

♦ *When will we meet?*

♦ *How often will we meet?* Meeting weekly or every other week is best if you can manage it. William Riley remarks, "Meetings once a month are too distant from each other for the threads of the last session not to be lost" (*The Bible Study Group: An Owner's Manual*).

♦ *How long will each meeting run?*

♦ *Where will we meet?*

♦ *Is any setup needed?* Christine Dodd writes that "the problem with meeting in a place like a church hall is that it can be very soul-destroying," given the cold, impersonal feel of many church facilities. If you have to meet in a church facility, Dodd recommends doing something to make the area homey (*Making Scripture Work*).

♦ *Who will host the meetings?* Leaders and hosts are not necessarily the same people.

♦ *Will we have refreshments?* Who will provide them? Don Cousins and Judson Poling make this recommendation: "Serve refreshments if you like, but save snacks and other foods for the end of the meeting to minimize distractions" (*Leader's Guide 1*).

♦ *What about child care?* Most experienced leaders of Bible discussion groups discourage bringing infants or other children to adult Bible discussions.

Agree on leadership. You need someone to facilitate—to keep the discussion on track, to see that everyone has a chance to speak, to help the group stay on schedule. Rena Duff, editor of the newsletter *Sharing God's Word Today,* recommends having two or three people take turns leading the discussions.

It's okay if the leader is not an expert on the Bible. You have this Six Weeks book as a guide, and if questions come up that no one can answer, you can delegate a participant to do a little research between meetings. Perhaps your parish priest or someone on the pastoral staff of your parish could offer advice. Or help may be available from your diocesan catechetical office or a local Catholic college or seminary.

It's important for the leader to set an example of listening, to draw out the quieter members (and occasionally restrain the more vocal ones), to move the group on when it gets stuck, to get the group back on track when the discussion moves away from the topic, and to restate and summarize what the group is learning. Sometimes the leader needs to remind the members of their agreements. An effective group leader is enthusiastic about the topic and the discussions and sets an example of learning from others and of using resources for growing in understanding.

As a discussion group matures, other members of the group will increasingly share in doing all these things on their own initiative.

Bible discussion is an opportunity to experience the fulfillment of Jesus' promise "Where two or three are gathered in my name, I am there among them" (Matthew 18:20). Put your discussion group in Jesus' hands. Pray for the guidance of the Spirit. And have a great time exploring God's word together!

Suggestions for Individuals

You can use this book just as well for individual study as for group discussion. While discussing the Bible with other people can be a rich experience, there are advantages to reading on your own. For example:

♦ You can focus on the points that interest you most.

♦ You can go at your own pace.

♦ You can be completely relaxed and unashamedly honest in your answers to all the questions, since you don't have to share them with anyone!

My suggestions for using this book on your own are these:

♦ Don't skip "Questions to Begin." The questions can help you as an individual reader warm up to the topic of the reading.

♦ Take your time on "Questions for Careful Reading" and "Questions for Application." While a group will probably not have enough time to work on all the questions, you can allow yourself the time to consider all of them if you are using the book by yourself.

♦ After reading "Guide to the Reading," go back and reread the Scripture text before answering the Questions for Application.

♦ Take the time to look up all the parenthetical Scripture references in the introduction, the Guides to the Reading, and the other material.

♦ Since you control the pace, give yourself plenty of opportunities to reflect on the meaning of the Scripture passages for you. Let your reading be an opportunity for these words to become God's words to you.

Resources

Bibles

The following editions of the Bible contain the full set of biblical books recognized by the Catholic Church, along with a great deal of useful explanatory material:

♦ The Catholic Study Bible (Oxford University Press), which uses the text of the New American Bible
♦ The Catholic Bible: Personal Study Edition (Oxford University Press), which also uses the text of the New American Bible
♦ The New Jerusalem Bible, the regular (not the reader's) edition (Doubleday)

Books, Web Sites, and Other Resources

♦ Kevin E. McKenna, *A Concise Guide to Catholic Social Teaching* (Notre Dame, IN: Ave Maria Press, 2002).
♦ Janet I. Miller, *Catechizing for Justice* (San Jose, CA: Resource Publications, 2001).
♦ Thomas Massaro, *Living Justice: Catholic Social Teaching in Action* (Franklin, WI: Sheed & Ward, 2000).
♦ Walter Brueggemann, *The Prophetic Imagination* (Minneapolis: Fortress Press, 2001).
♦ Walter Brueggemann, *Hopeful Imagination: Prophetic Voices in Exile* (Philadelphia: Fortress Press, 1986).
♦ Carroll Stuhlmueller, *Amos, Hosea, Micah, Nahum, Zephaniah, Habakkuk* (Collegeville, MN: Liturgical Press, 1986).

How has Scripture had an impact on your life? Was this book helpful to you in your study of the Bible? Please send comments, suggestions, and personal experiences to Kevin Perrotta, General Editor, Editorial Department, Loyola Press, 3441 N. Ashland Ave., Chicago, IL 60657.